the flowers of eden

Poetry from
The Awakening Rose Collection, Volume 1

shayna rose

Copyright © 2025 Shayna Rose

All rights reserved. No part of this book may be reproduced or used in any manner without the prior written permission of the copyright owner, except for the use of brief quotations.

Happy to share content, for permission please contact the author at:
www.theawakeningrose.com

ISBN- 979-8-3306-2354-9 (Hardcover)

First hardcover edition February 2, 2025

Cover Design by Shayna Rose
Interior Design by Shayna Rose
Images and Art Courtesy of Lana Elanor

Printed by The Awakening Rose in the USA

For Nana,
The woman who taught me to
honor my ancestral roots.

For Momma,
The woman who taught me to
love the flowers around me.

For my husband,
The man who believed that this rose
was worthy of love.

For my daughter,
The child of flowers whose joy
sings with the heart of stars.

note to the reader

This book contains sensitive material that may evoke past traumas, including:

Sexual harm
Abuse
Self-Harm
Grief and Loss
Death and Mortality
Among others

Please remember to practice self-care, self-compassion, and above all, self-love. My hope is that you find comfort knowing that, while your experiences may be your own, you are never alone in your pain. My deepest longing is that together, we may begin to heal.

introduction

"Trees are the kindest things I know.
They do not harm, they simply grow,
And spread shade for sleepy cows
And gather birds among their branches."
-Shayna, age 6

This poetry collection was born from a place of unbearable sorrow and profound transformation. The Flowers of Eden is not only my story—it is the mirror of a shared experience, a reflection of what it means to navigate the world disconnected from yourself. It is the first step in The Awakening Rose Poetry Collection, a journey that moves from innocence to loss, from rejection to reclamation, and finally toward love and integration.

For much of my life, I rejected myself—my body, my worth, my voice. In that void, I allowed harm to take root: harm inflicted by others, and harm I unknowingly invited through my silence and self-abandonment. As I turned away from my body and my truth, I endured wounds from men and women alike, navigating a world that mirrored my disconnection.

This collection also holds the grief of losing my mother and my nana, two women who embodied kindness, shelter, and the quiet strength of growth. Their deaths left an unbearable void, and yet, in mourning them, I began to turn toward my ancestors, searching for meaning and solace in their stories. Like trees offering shade, their lives became a shelter for my own, guiding me through my pain.

This book reflects that journey: from the innocence of childhood to the wounds of betrayal and trauma, through the devastation of grief, and finally toward a reclamation of self. Its poems explore themes of motherhood, infertility, sexual harm, love, and resilience—universal truths that echo the experiences of women everywhere.

The Flowers of Eden is more than a reflection of pain; it is a story of transformation. It speaks to the courage required to sit with grief, to confront the shadows that haunt us, and to believe in love again. It is about the bravery to live fully, even after loss, and the faith that love—true love—transcends pain, sorrow, and even death.

My hope is that these words will resonate with your own story, offering a sense of connection, healing, and strength. May this book be the first step in your journey home, as it has been for me.

table of contents

sprout

the awakening rose 13

the flowers of eden 14

mother 16

gaia 17

roots 18

the family tree 19

flower song 20

buttercup 21

the golden poppy 22

sweet pea 23

morning glory 24

blush 25

clay 26

peony 28

delicate 29

loss of self 30

the seed 31

the wildflower 32

tulip 33

neglect 34

rejection 35

among sweeter flowers 36

wild belief 37

the warning 38

paradise lost 39

tree 41

stolen fruit 42

the apple 43

grow

passage 46

the garden path 47

dominate 48

domesticate 49

skin 50

pruned 51

shrinking violets 52

marigold 53

thorns 54

the oleander 55

temptation 56

belladonna 57

nectar 58

toxic 59

love me not 60

bed of flowers 61

sow 62

the nest 63

scars 64

quake 65

resilience 66

buried 67

trapped 68

shame 69

chasing butterflies 70

the dandelion 71

home body 72

the wallflower 73

hollow 74

plucked 75

grave 76

leaves of gold 77

willow 78

the aspen 79

falling leaves 80

bloom

rise 85

persist 86

reach 87

climb 88

the desert rose 89

lavender 90

rowan 91

perfume 92

lily 93

to bloom 94

the clover *95*

tender *96*

touch *97*

the forest *98*

unravel *99*

spine *100*

botanical bodies *101*

the tree of time *102*

the tree of knowledge *103*

aster *104*

lotus *105*

rosa mundi *106*

the redwoods *107*

the garden *108*

eden *110*

spirits of the land *111*

the tree of life *112*

autumn bodies *113*

home *114*

bury me *115*

at lands' end *116*

the fruit *117*

familiar face *118*

soil *119*

life song *120*

the moon gate *121*

the flowers of eden

shayna rose

the awakening rose

*On the horizon about to ignite
A day that brings a pure light,
Finally ending this long, dark night.*

*In a garden where many a flower grows
I am just one small, little rose,
Filled with the longings our collective heart knows.*

*This is the moment we dreamed of
As we turn our face to the light above
Soaking in the shine of this great love.*

*Can you feel our souls synchronizing?
Blooming together in a form so mesmerizing
Can't you see: there is an awakening rising.*

the flowers of eden

a villanelle

The stars of heaven fell from the night
Planting themselves within Eden's womb,
Longing to share the glow of their bright light.

To sprout they had to put up a fight
Pushing against their fear and their gloom
The stars of heaven fell from the night.

They used all their strength in their plight
To ensure that the soil would not be their tomb,
Longing to share the glow of their bright light.

From the earth, these stars took new height
Reborn as flora the soil chose to exhume
The stars of heaven fell from the night.

These flowers carried great joy and divine sprite
And together they unleashed their sweet perfume,
Longing to share the glow of their bright light.

And these flowers were a beautiful sight
Unfolding love within their glorious bloom
The stars of heaven fell from the night,
Longing to share the glow of their bright light.

shayna rose

the flowers of eden

mother

a villanelle

Oh, Great Mother, how I have forsaken you
I ignored your cries and your pleas
As I chose to run away from the only love I knew.

I could not face what I knew to be true
I was so unsettled with unease
Oh, Great Mother, how I have forsaken you

I hope you know I had no clue
That my actions would lead to such dis-ease
As I chose to run away from the only love I knew.

Everything seemed so outside my view
I cannot even look at what the mirror sees
Oh, Great Mother, how I have forsaken you

Too late I realized what your love could do
That they had the power to soothe tears like these
As I chose to run away from the only love I knew.

I am sorry for what I have put you through
I am praying for forgiveness, begging on my knees
Oh, Great Mother, how I have forsaken you
As I chose to run away from the only love I knew.

gaia

a quatern

Within Mother Gaia's great womb
We are destined to live and bloom
Too short are we to embrace
For her babies grow at rapid pace.

A terrible truth will linger and loom
Within Mother Gaia's great womb
That her babies will live quicker
And their life flame will flicker.

Knowing it is only short years
Before she is again in tears
Within Mother Gaia's great womb
Her babies will be met with doom.

We will reunite after we die
For life is a blink of an eye
We will rest forever in our tomb
Within Mother Gaia's great womb.

the flowers of eden

roots

a triolet

Ancestor, what a flower you were-
Blooming in the same sun but many springs ago
But to time and memory, you are just a blur
Ancestor, what a flower you were-
Your roots still act as a gentle whisper
Because of you many more flowers were to grow
Ancestor, what a flower you were-
Blooming in the same sun but many springs ago.

shayna rose

the family tree

a nonet

Years long gone away, far from today
Hang upon a great canopy:
Heirlooms weave through centuries
Unclear how long they last
For this tree may die
As I may be
The last of
My blood
Line.

the flowers of eden

flower song

a haiku

A flower's heart beats
With the rhythm of longing
Alive with love songs.

shayna rose

buttercup

a triolet

The buttercups frolic in the summer sun
Taking joy in simply being alive
Giggling in the breeze, their worries undone
The buttercups frolic in the summer sun
Bringing laughter, play, and endless fun
Never dulling their shine when dark clouds arrive
The buttercups frolic in the summer sun
Taking joy in simply being alive.

the flowers of eden

the golden poppy

She was one perky poppy,
Clothed in the colors
Of the California sun—
And her heart of gold
Radiated with the song of joy.

for shelby

shayna rose

---

sweet pea

a tercet

A quiet and shy little flower; sweet and never sour
The Sweet Pea hangs her love onto thee
Her heart is one which you never wish to part.

for shelby

the flowers of eden

---

morning glory

In the morning, she arose with radiance,
She unfolded her petals with a great sigh
And with her morning bloom
She graced the air with the scent of Zen.

blush

When Heaven's purest rose
Took a sip from the wine of love
Her petals blushed with color
Drunk on this sweet feeling,
Bold with the desire of another.

the flowers of eden

clay

A quatern

If I could sculpt myself from clay
I would be sculpted in a different way
I am certainly not what the Artist saw fit
Clearly there was a detail that was omit

What could I be, I can not say
If I could sculpt myself from clay
The Artist crafted a mistake
Only seen after the clay had baked

How could I correct this mess
I cannot help but obsess
If I could sculpt myself from clay
It would be beauty that I would convey

Yet, the Artist knew how to craft me
In the way I was meant to be
What divine action I would betray
If I could sculpt myself from clay

shayna rose

the flowers of eden

peony

We learn so often to hide ourselves away
Trying to keep the critics at bay;
Under layers and layers of "beauty"
Women are required to this duty:
To be flawless and perfect
An illusion we so often try to depict
Like a peony, we are afraid to simply be
In case you don't like the face you see.

shayna rose

delicate

Sometimes we hold ourselves as delicate flowers
Our petals beautiful and bright
Hoping to be loved and appreciated
Yet hiding our hearts beneath our superficial charm.
Because what if our unique scent is not alluring,
But others find unbearably revolting.

the flowers of eden

loss of self

Her sense of self was fleeting
And like the delicate dandelion,
She would lose parts of herself
And watch them float away into the sky.

shayna rose

the seed

a rondel

Just like the seed,
I need to break
So that when I wake
I can be freed.

I let my hope take the lead
It is my fears I forsake
Just like the seed
I need to break.

There are dreams I must feed
I cannot ignore this hungered ache
Change creates a unsettling quake,
My desire begins to bleed,
Just like the seed
I need to break.

the flowers of eden

---

the wildflower

She wanted to live wild
Among the flowers
Bathing in the shine
Of the loving sun,
Far from any poacher's eye
Because she knew that
Humans have a tendency
To pick on beautiful blooms
And that plucked flowers always die.

tulip

Listen to the lovely Tulip's advice:
Your own individuality you need not sacrifice
When blooming alongside another flower
Trust that you are blessed with much power
Do not wear the worries on your head
Drifting in your thoughts before bed;
Other women wear confidence like a crown
That should not bring your spirit down
Just because many lovely flowers are seen
Doesn't mean you cannot be a queen.

the flowers of eden

neglect

I knew how to care:
I cared for all the people
I cared for all the animals
I cared for all the plants
I cared for all the things
That was what I was good at
But I never knew how to care
For myself.

I deprived myself of so much
Pushed away thoughts
Swallowed my feelings
Ridiculed my body
Condemned my actions
Instead of flourishing as others do,
I chose not to care for my needs
To the point where I withered away
And I fell into neglect.

rejection

When we pull away in fear of love,
We plant a seed deep into the heart.
The pain sprouts quickly
And Love's flowers tire,
Wilted, hanging in despair.
In this garden, it is not the weeds
That roam wild,
But instead, the belief that
One can never be loved.

the flowers of eden

among sweeter flowers

Some days she was the rose;
The Queen of the Garden
With an army of thorns at her defense.

Other days, she was the silver dandelion;
A weed among sweeter flowers
And she would fall apart at the slightest touch.

wild belief

Her petals were plucked by her own hand,
Her head hangs, wilted and withered,
All because a belief grew wild in her heart:
That she wasn't really a flower,
But merely a worthless weed.

the flowers of eden

the warning

a nonet

In the pit of my stomach, there is
A *flurry of bells a-ringing*
Warning me of a danger
Lurking beyond my sight
Like a predator,
Fate moves swiftly
Set to pounce
On its
Prey.

paradise lost

We *played among the flowers*
In the Garden of Ignorant Bliss.
Like the fog rolling over our sweet sun,
The knowledge of death
Sits in the pit of our stomach
Like rotting fruit from a forbidden tree.
And just like the children: Eve and her Adam,
And Juliet and her Romeo,
The color of the flowers fade around us
And the world's true colors begin to show:
We are left with our hope for joy,
The pulls of our sorrow,
And the world becomes a barren place
For our lonely souls.

the flowers of eden

tree

If you ever heard a tree
Exhale its last breath of life,
You may not escape the knowledge
That an axe is just a butcher's knife.

the flowers of eden

stolen fruit

This little Cherry Tree
Wore a spring gown
Laced with pink blossoms
And her fruit was sweetened
By her trusting heart.
But her love was stolen
Causing her fruit to sour.
Her petals fell away, ashamed
Replaced by bleeding red leaves
That slowly turned black in mourning
For she grieved the loss of her innocence
That would never return.

shayna rose

the apple

What of the sweet apple
At the surface, crisp juicy
But at the core laced with poison.
What of both the desire and fear
That lurk within all things
Residing outside the gates of Eden.

the flowers of eden

shayna rose

grow

the flowers of eden

passage

a palindrome

Ignorance
Walks the road away from
Our greater connection to God that
Within the unraveling cosmic tapestry
We dangle between desire and fear,
Being starved for knowledge,
And never are we
Knowing who we truly are
We walk always
Between the thread of birth and death
Knowing that heaven is
Out of reach
The light is never
Brighter than the shadow
That consumes our soul
And knowing that truth is something
Beyond all understanding,
Just outside what is considered
The path of love
Blooming everlasting toward
Enlightenment

(read in reverse)

shayna rose

the garden path

an idiom poem

You have led me up the garden path,
Save your flowery words for someone else,
I am exhausted from shrinking like a violet
As you cut up heads of poppies in your wake
I would rather take a kiss from the oleander
And push up the daisies whilst I sleep
Than to be your lovely little geranium.

the flowers of eden

dominate

a triolet

He *picked the sacred flower,*
And *the garden wilted around him-*
Because he thought it was within his power,
He *picked the sacred flower,*
And he did not even cower
When the world grew instantly grim.
He *picked the sacred flower,*
And *the garden wilted around him.*

shayna rose

domesticate

Floral Maidens
Are just flowers plucked by
The hands of men.
These wildflowers cannot be tamed
Yet their spirits wither from the stale air
And the lack of sunshine.
When they can no longer
Access the spirit
That sings in harmony
With the song of earth,
Their hearts hum dully
In flat tunes
Behind the bars
Of their cages,
Crying to be free.

the flowers of eden

skin

When I *feel*
Objectified,
Scrutinized,
Judged;
I *wish that I could*
Peel my skin
Off my soul
And run away
Where the naked eye
Cannot find me.

shayna rose

pruned

They called it pruning
When they cut pieces
Of me away.
They said that if I let
These parts of me die
That I would become beautiful -
But their shears
Kept cutting and cutting
And soon all the things
That I once liked about myself
Were gone
And I forgot
That I was once a flower
In bloom.

the flowers of eden

shrinking violets

a triolet

Shrinking violets are not to blame
If the world cannot accept them
Too long they have held their shame –
Shrinking violets are not to blame
When the world is obsessed with fame –
They carry their burdens at the stem
Shrinking violets are not to blame
If the world cannot accept them.

marigold

a triolet

It *didn't matter that she was made of gold,*
Jealousy turned this marigold's heart green.
The sight of another flower turned her blood cold
It *didn't matter that she was made of gold,*
And nor did all the compliments she was told
She was the only one who could be Queen
It *didn't matter that she was made of gold,*
Jealousy turned this marigold's heart green.

the flowers of eden

thorns

She had been handled
And touched
And grabbed at
Without her consent –
Her soft petals vulnerable
To the paws of predators.
The sensations of man
Were delighted and tickled
With this beauty,
And she had no choice
But to harden herself with thorns
To keep the desires of men
At bay.

shayna rose

the oleander

We think of Death with his sickle,
Cutting the flowers at the stem without care
His black robes causing our skin to prickle,
And his darkness blocks the light of the sun's stare.

But Death can take a form without need to cower
Instead, she can lure you in with her beauty
Wrapped in petals of an Oleander flower:
Sweet and innocent, and yet incredibly deadly.

the flowers of eden

temptation

a palindrome

Desire
Just the alluring seduction of
The sweet lie
Of this ripe fruit,
Just a bite
I won't tell, it is
Just a little secret
Until you find yourself with
Endless, lingering shame
Numbing with the state of
Fear

(read in reverse)

belladonna

Belladonna, I see you eyeing a lover
One whose heart belongs to another
Oh darling, I see you playing coy
This is the game you most enjoy –
A dark fantasy lingers behind your eyes
Your true intentions, you disguise
You are a dart through the heart
But your devil's arrow is not one to tear apart
The bonds that true love has sewn
And it will be you who will be alone.

I see you setting your snare
Not giving one ounce of care
That this prize does not belong to you
I urge you to get lost, boo
Your attempt to control the body of this man
Is the most futile plan
You must know, you are not welcome here
And what you fail to see, dear
There are men who know such
That not all flowers are safe to touch.

the flowers of eden

nectar

The flower of woman was potent;
For any man who fell drunk upon the nectar
Within this flower's delicate petals
Became powerless to its entrapment.
For the price to rise to the Heavens
Was often the fall of kingdoms.

toxic

When sweet turns sour
A tickle's laugh turns to tears
And wine slowly turns to poison
The things that will kill us
Are often the things we long most for

the flowers of eden

love me not

*He believed he was the sun,
And when he walked through the garden,
All the flowers stood tall
Basking in his charm.
In the wake of his cold shadow,
The flowers pulled at their own petals
With the question
Of whether he loved them
Or not.*

shayna rose

bed of flowers

He was reckless in his affection and care
It was lust, not love, he wanted to share
So fickle his attentions were for me
And it took me too long to see
That the truth I came to most dread:
Is that I wasn't the only flower in his bed.

the flowers of eden

sow

He was reckless
Sowing his seed in many fertile soil –
He fathered many a faceless babe
Who were tricked with a taste of tansy
And whose lives never bloomed
Outside the womb.

shayna rose

the nest

Within her was a nest
That held these fragile eggs,
Like the seeds of a pomegranate.
Each were irreplaceable
And every one of them held
The most ancient magic.
Yet too often,
These beautiful beauties would break
And cause her womb to weep;
Succumbing to great heartbreak
Mourning the death of something
That was never truly alive.

the flowers of eden

scars

*I have scars on my womb
Where death touched me
From whence I bled
Over and over
With the tears of grief,
And the loss of hope,
From where
Life ceased to grow
Within me.*

shayna rose

quake

A rumbling quake breaks me open wide,
A wound that is too great to hide
I fall back into this ancient womb
Buried, alone, forever in this dark tomb.

the flowers of eden

resilience

A seed of life –
Buried before it is birthed
A seed of dreams –
Sleeps before it awakens
A seed of hope –
Blooms within darkness.

shayna rose

buried

Like the seed,
The hardest part of growing
Happens when we think
We are alone,
Buried in the dark,
Struggling to see the light.

the flowers of eden

trapped

Trapped within my body,
Lies a dark secret.
For all the harms
Inflicted by the hands of others
Linger beneath the surface of my skin
These acts planted datura flowers;
These little trauma trumpets
Howl with unresolved pain
Trapped within my body.

shayna rose

shame

a rondel

It was shame that stained my skin,
And I wanted to find a way to hide
And no mattered how hard I tried
Shame would always win.

No one really cares what's within
Since outward beauty is how we lied
It was shame that stained my skin
And I wanted to find a way to hide.

It only made sense to become a shut-in
Because others refused to be blind-eyed
Feigning invisibility was how I replied
When the world expects you to be dignified
It was shame that stained my skin.

the flowers of eden

chasing butterflies

In my childhood,
I spent my time listening to the trees,
Counting petals on the flowers,
And chasing butterflies.
I don't know when that part of me died
But what I do know is that now
I spend my time listening to complaints,
Counting the hours of the day,
And chasing after the approval of others.
I miss the garden of my childhood
And the friendly faces that were there.

shayna rose

the dandelion

A dandelion breathes into this field
A thousand wishes waiting to be revealed.
A field of love and of possibility,
Surrendering to graceful vulnerability.

A dandelion cries in this field
A grief much too large to shield.
A field of heartbreak and of sorrow,
Holding onto hope for tomorrow.

A dandelion in this field
Shows a strength we all can wield.
In a field of both sunshine and rain,
A dandelion can only create from its pain.

the flowers of eden

home body

My body was always a place of safety
But I reluctantly turned away
Finding solace in others
Who would eventually betray.
Seeing that there was no home
Outside of this skin
I tried to find a way back in
But my body was tired, worn, and thin
And denied me all the comforts I longed for
I wished I had learned this lesson before
Because my body is not home anymore
And in this world, there is no place like home
For you can search, seek, and roam
But finding peace within yourself
Is truly the only place you can call home.

the wallflower

a sonnet

She was a pretty little flower,
Yet far too often, she faded into the wall
Because she could not hold her head tall
And she gave away all her power.

She believed that from grace she would fall,
A misstep would cause her to quiver and cower
Because she believed she turned all the fruit sour
And she could never see the truth at all.

Within her heart, she began to nourish
An aching will to grow and thrive
Only then, did she see how her perfume
Caused hearts around her to flourish
Inspiring others around her to come alive,
It was her love of others that made her bloom.

the flowers of eden

hollow

a tyburn

Hollow.
Empty.
Taken.
Stolen.
This body is now hollow, empty
By death's hand: a soul taken, stolen.

shayna rose

plucked

*You bloomed for a lifetime
Until Death came to pluck you
From the garden of life.
Despite being a single flower
In the world's garden,
Your absence is felt
Every single day
And your fragrant memory
Still lingers upon the hearts
Of all those who loved you.
There will be a day
When Death will pluck me away
And I will join you
Outside the garden walls
And beyond the seasons of life.*

the flowers of eden

grave

a quatern

An empty void just six feet deep
Only winter rains fill this hole
Overflowing with great sorrow
The showering of endless grief.

This grave dirt cannot turn nor churn
An empty void just six feet deep
What death can plant in this great grief:
A hopeful seed, destined to drown.

The snowdrops mourn with tears of rain
For when love is severed by death
An empty void just six feet deep
Is what will remain in its place.

What can grow from death, but we hope
That there will be a way to touch
Love again and death is not
An empty void just six feet deep.

leaves of gold

The leaves glow in copper and gold
In honor of the dying Sun.
The trees offer their treasures
And lay them at the feet of Mother Earth,
To grant safe passage for the Sun
And his journey into the underworld.

willow

Oh Willow, Willow by the lake
Teach me to bend, but not to break
For my heart cannot take
The weight of this loss, I cannot shake.

Oh Willow, Willow by the lake
Help me soothe this incredible ache
My heart sits in dark waiting for day to break
Without your help, I fear I may never wake.

Oh Willow, Willow by the lake
There has been an incredible mistake
Love turned to grief swiftly like the bite of a snake
How can we love, knowing what's at stake?
Please Mother Willow, ease my pain for love's sake.

the aspen

Like when the winds of change
Cause the Aspen to tremble,
I feel a threat at the core of my being
And I worry my hopes and dreams
Will fade away as they sail away
Across the Ocean of Stars,
Far from my reach.
Who am I in it all?
Will this storm be my downfall?
I seek my ancestors for guidance
Asking them to shield me from pain,
To ground me with their deep roots,
And to allow me to stand firm knowing
That I am more than these struggles
That parts of me can die
And I will be able to live again.

the flowers of eden

falling leaves

Oh darling, I hope you will see
That all the things you are letting go
Is like how the tree
Parts with its leaves.
Allow your own leaves to fall
With grace and ease
And welcome that long needed
Rest of winter.
In time, spring will come
And just like the tree,
You will bloom once again.

shayna rose

the flowers of eden

shayna rose

bloom

the flowers of eden

shayna rose

rise

Dormant seeds lie in a grave
Holding a blueprint of a great design
They sleep until conditions are ripe
And they rise, rise, rise
With the hope of new life.

the flowers of eden

persist

She grew and she grew
In lands said to be infertile,
She grew
In places uninhabitable
She grew
She grew and she grew
Through all the harsh conditions
Through all the negative words
Through all the hate
She grew.

shayna rose

reach

a quatern

For aren't we all just hopeful flowers
Reaching for the stars in the sky
We seek to grow tall as towers
To grasp that love which mystifies

To reach the great heavens above
For aren't we all just hopeful flowers
Thinking the price to pay for love:
Trade our body for lust's power

Who can know what lust devours
Because when you are in its hand
For aren't we all just hopeful flowers
Destined to be buried in sand

Who but love was to teach
That affection will shower
The stars will now be within reach
For aren't we all just hopeful flowers

the flowers of eden

climb

Her soul was drenched in sweet sweat
From all she invested in herself
She stretched beyond her body
She grew taller than she ever imagined,
Climbing towards the sky
Because she believed that one day
She would fly.

shayna rose

the desert rose

What is this bloom
That arises from the desert floor
A sweetness plumes across the barren land
A flower that resists succumbing to
The ashes of death
But thrives where the ground is parched of love
She, herself, a child of hope;
A beauty that permeates love:
My sweet desert rose.

for clemance

the flowers of eden

lavender

When life carries a great weight
That our senses struggle to sedate
There is hope that we can render
As Lavender sings with surrender.

Why is it hard to settle our bones
When they weigh heavy as stones,
We can mend with a touch so tender
As Lavender sings with surrender.

Let us choose to exhale with relief
And our hearts can release our grief
To take a moment soaked with splendor
As Lavender sings with surrender.

rowan

Mother Rowan, ablaze with Divine Fire
Whisper to me the secrets beyond the senses
Please share with me the truth behind
This fiery flame of life
Please tell me what lies beyond
The whisper of the soul
Where the spirits sing with light.

the flowers of eden

perfume

What of love's sweet perfume
With its scent it can make
A man go mad with lust,
A mother grow heavy with grief,
And a soul to live on forever.

lily

a triolet

What a lily teaches me
Is to surrender to love all the way
So that I can fully see
What a lily teaches me.
For that love sets the soul free
And not even death can take our love away.
What a lily teaches me
Is to surrender to love all the way.

for lillie

the flowers of eden

to bloom

The most beautiful flowers
In the garden of the world
Are those with the hearts
That choose to bloom
With their radiant love.

shayna rose

the clover

a villanelle

From the moment I knew that it was he,
The clovers sprang whenever he came near –
I just knew he was always meant for me

Life became soft and a bit carefree
And ladybirds would often appear
From the moment I knew that it was he

His arms were like branches of a great tree
A place I knew I could shelter year after year
I just knew he was always meant for me

Something deep inside me had been set free
And I reveled in how much his love was sincere
From the moment I knew that it was he

When he is near, my heart is filled with glee
My love for him brings the stars to cheer
I just knew he was always meant for me

The stubborn Fates would agree
And no outside forces would interfere
From the moment I knew that it was he
I just knew he was always meant for me

for ron

the flowers of eden

tender

Tender is his gentle touch –
He caresses the deepest parts of my soul,
And my body unfolds and blooms
At the very sight of him.

for ron

shayna rose

touch

There was something wild
About the way we touched –
Like bees getting drunk
On a flowers pollen
Love filled us up
From top to bottom.

for ron

the flowers of eden

the forest

I *want to soak*
In *the colors of the sunset*
And run away
Into the depths of the forest.

I *need to rest now,*
For the daggers stuck in my back
Are slowly killing me
From the intimate bonds
Who have betrayed my trust.

If I am to die misunderstood,
Let it still be with a heart full of love
And compassion for those
Who have drawn their weapons against me.

I surrender my last breath to the forest
And the trees sing me softly
To that sacred sleep.
When I wake again,
I hope to soak in the colors of the sunrise
And live in peace amongst the trees.

shayna rose

unravel

*From the noise of the city, I flee
Taking in the sanctuary of the trees
For they are silent hosts.
They embrace me as my thoughts unravel
Like strings they get caught in the branches
These friends don't judge or criticize
For the mental waste I have unleashed
Instead, they take the thoughts left unspun
And slowly weave the threads back
Piece by piece
Into a warm tapestry
Holding me close
With silent comfort.*

the flowers of eden

spine

My soul pulls on my skin,
Zips it up from the spine,
Tethering to the bones of this body
Then falls into a deep sleep for a lifetime
Dreaming of the world as we see it
Consumed by an identity
We spend our life crafting
And forgetting who we truly are.

botanical bodies

What little we know of our botanical bodies:
Dressed in flesh,
Yet flowers behind a façade
Drowning in light from
The far-reaching sun.

What little we know of our botanical bodies:
How fragmented we've become
For we know not what we truly are.

the flowers of eden

the tree of time

It is said that time is an arrow
Flying in one direction
Towards the end of eternity.
But time is not an arrow,
Instead, time is the branches
Of a great Yew Tree.
With every moment that passes,
It grows great with wisdom,
Spanning space with its branches.
And only God can rest
Under the canopy of
The Tree of Time.

shayna rose

the tree of knowledge

a pantoum

Since the Wise Tree was cut down
Its pages were fastened into a book
All the ripe fruit had turned brown
Knowledge is what we thought we took

Its pages were fastened into a book
With words beyond what we can read
Knowledge is what we thought we took –
But really all we had was greed

With words beyond what we can read
We think we know, but we are lost
But really all we had was greed
And we don't know what it will cost

We think we know, but we are lost
All the ripe fruit had turned brown
And we don't know what it will cost
Since the Wise Tree was cut down

the flowers of eden

aster

And so, the truth is told of how we came to be:
It was Father Sky who fell in love with Mother Earth
And the seed he planted was the gift of life:
From the ground, a flower bloomed like a star
Born of the earth and of the sky.

shayna rose

lotus

What arises from the murky waters below
Like Aphrodite rises from the sea foam
A flower that sings with the love of God
Unfolding in bloom and rising to the sky
The lotus song sings
Within the heart of all
For what lies beyond enlightenment
Is pure love.

rosa mundi

a villanelle

There is a secret at the heart of all
Greater than what hails from above
Because we heed a greater call

Because that what flies can fall
Even that which seems pure as a dove
There is a secret at the heart of all

When the task at hand is hardly small
Sometimes we need a bit of a shove
Because we heed a greater call

This greater truth will enthrall
Eve, Isis, Diana, and Mary are all a part of
There is a secret at the heart of all

For finding the light beyond nightfall
Our hidden truth lays hereof
Because we heed a greater call

This greater purpose for us to befall
Is of Rosa Mundi, the spirit of love
The secret at the heart of all
Because we heed a greater call

shayna rose

the redwoods

*There in the forest,
In the cathedral of the Redwoods
A collective chant rises to the heavens
In a soft hum of harmony
As the trees sing as one:
A song too delicate for the ears
But can be heard with the soul.*

the flowers of eden

the garden

a sestina

There is a great garden
Home to all the flowers
Gracefully unfolding in bloom
Tended with care so delicate
In order to give rise to love
And to breathe with life.

What a great gift that is life
Held in the womb of our earthly garden
Nourished by unconditional love-
Don't we see that our flowers
Are reminders that life is so delicate
That we shouldn't be afraid to bloom.

And yet so many of us are hesitant to bloom
We do not get another chance at this life
Knowing that our mortality is so delicate –
We can only take solace in the peace of the garden
Only to believe in the kindness of flowers
And the great power of love.

Only when we surrender our being to love
Can we allow our full selves to bloom:
To become the loveliest of the flowers
Because we have honored our life,
So, when we bloom so does the rest of the garden
And we can hold ourselves more than delicate.

shayna rose

Yet our bodies, our hearts, and our lives are delicate
Healed by the light of love –
While we can run away from the garden,
We know that it is with others that we bloom
For being alone is not the purpose of life
Instead, we are meant to dance among the flowers.

The glory of all Eden's flowers
Is a strength resting behind a facade so delicate –
To surrender to a fully lived life
That carries the scent of love
With the courage to bloom
To take its rightful place in the garden.

What a life lived among the flowers
A home in a garden so delicate
Where only love can bloom.

the flowers of eden

eden

Beyond the groves of green,
An Eden is waiting to be seen
So much we cannot see with our eyes
We cannot recognize this great prize:
A harp of holly
Singing without folly
Unappreciated by our mortal ears
For too little a sound it hears.
This world is filled with wonder
With delights our mind cannot ponder
When will we calm our nerves
And honor what our Earth deserves
This, our garden, full of grace
With magic our senses cannot trace.

shayna rose

spirits of the land

*Within the great garden
Are the spirits of the land
With the past buried beneath our feet
And seeds of the future
With many flowers yet to bloom.*

the flowers of eden

the tree of life

I am just a small bloom
Gracing this Great Tree
For I will spend one season of life
Hanging from its branches.
Life is a swift jab from the Ash,
Life is to bleed like the Alder
But from the core my pain,
I have found healing in the Willow.
As a prize of being loves sweet bride,
I wore a crown made of Hawthorn sprigs
As a mother of future blooms,
I made a nest of Oak leaves
As an aging crone whose face transformed
Like the trunk of an Old Yew
And when my season has come and gone
I will be buried alongside
The roots of Redwood Family
And I will be reunited with my ancestors
Somewhere beyond the sunset.

shayna rose

autumn bodies

Her soul shone bright at sunset,
As she wore her long life with grace
And like the tree loses its leaves,
She surrendered the past
To the autumn wind
And her eyes twinkled
With the arrival
Of the first stars in heaven.

As Heaven's sky fills
With the echoes of stars
The keepers of time
And the witness of history.
She was reminded of
All those who came before:
What a reunion to behold
Our lost loves wait for thee
Beyond the light of love.

What are our autumn years
But a time of acceptance
And a time for peace.

the flowers of eden

home

I *long for my home*
The one I *cannot return to*
Where *my family tree rests its roots*
Alongside *the bodies of my ancestors*
My *past lingers alive in this land*
But *my future remains untethered*
Maybe *one day, I will return*
And *my ancestors will sing with joy*
That I *have come home*

shayna rose

bury me

Bury me under a bed of roses
Let my bones grow into their bushes
And let my soul bloom again
Under the radiant sun
With the memory of my love.

the flowers of eden

at lands' end

a pantoum

Do we know what lies beyond Land's End
Shrouded by the veil lingering at the edge
To dare to believe that we can transcend
The leap our souls must prepare to fledge

Shrouded by the veil lingering at the edge
We make our way towards the field of reeds
The leap our souls must prepare to fledge
Onward to where Eden sows her precious seeds

We make our way towards the field of reeds
Our souls make way towards the setting sun
Onward to where Eden sows her precious seeds
Our physical bodies and senses are but none

Our souls make way towards the setting sun
To dare to believe that we can transcend
Our physical bodies and senses are but none
Do we know what lies beyond Land's End?

shayna rose

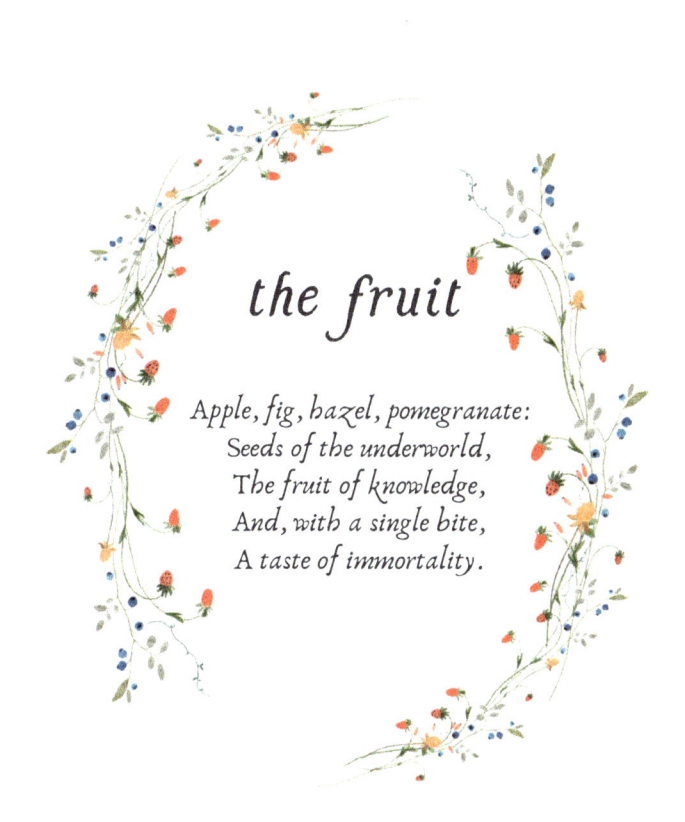

the fruit

Apple, fig, hazel, pomegranate:
Seeds of the underworld,
The fruit of knowledge,
And, with a single bite,
A taste of immortality.

the flowers of eden

familiar face

I waited a lifetime to see her face
I couldn't know for certain
What form it would take
But at first glance I knew
She was so familiar
As if I have seen her every day.

for clara

soil

Her eyes are like soil
They carry the stories
And the bones of our ancestors,
They hold the dreams
And the seeds of our descendants.
She is the Earth,
She is the Spring,
She is the Past,
And she is the Future.

for clara

the flowers of eden

life song

And from the tree of life,
A *flute was carved*
It *sang with joy*
It *sang with sorrow*
And with all the hope and fears
That lay between.

The *flute vibrates with the*
Rhythm of thought
And the life song
Echoing across the
Ocean of the universe
And the seas of time.

shayna rose

the moon gate

a rondel

Follow me through the gate of the moon,
Just east of the garden, facing the rising sun
Where the world of matter comes undone
Where energy sings with its unique tune.

On the other side, our hearts will swoon
And its beauty and peace will stun
Follow me through the gate of the moon,
Just east of the garden, facing the rising sun

Join me where your journey has only begun;
From our bodies away we prune
And time won't end too soon,
Where you are reunited with all as one
Follow me through the gate of the moon.

the flowers of eden

shayna rose

The journey continues
Beyond the gates of the garden
Where we heed a greater call
One that breathes with

the song of the sky

the flowers of eden

appreciation

Firstly, this book would not have been possible without my nana and my momma. I am eternally grateful for the love you gave me and the powerful, raw feminine energy you both carried throughout your lives. While our relationships weren't always easy, the love we shared was unwavering, a constant thread that binds us.

To my husband: You have reignited my heart and my creativity. You are my muse, my unwavering support, and my greatest believer, even when I'm paralyzed by self-doubt. Words will never fully capture how much I love you, but I'll spend my life finding ways to show you.

To my dad, my brother, and my sister: Thank you for keeping me grounded and connected to the world. Your humor pulls me back when I take life too seriously, and your unwavering support reminds me I'm never alone.

To my Irish aunts, uncles, and cousins: You've always embraced me and reminded me of who I truly am. Your hearts are a home I can always return to when I lose myself in the world. Thank you for your endless encouragement and love.

Lastly, to my coach, Ranya: Without you, the true me would still be buried in the dark. You helped me uncover my potential and see myself clearly. Thank you for guiding me back to who I really am.

I love you all.

the flowers of eden

about shayna

As an extremely imaginative child, Shayna often found herself lost in worlds beyond our reality; some would say she would drift off in a dream, and others said she lived in fantasy. Nevertheless, Shayna was always in touch with something just beyond the physical world, connected deeply to her emotions and the emotions of others, and often found her own world to be an escape from the overstimulation of life. As a child, she was highly creative, dabbling in arts and poetry. Her notebooks were filled with verses and sketches, safe havens where her inner world could flourish. But as adulthood swept in, the pragmatic demands of life brought Shayna out of fantasy and into practicality. She threw her dreams away, and almost overnight her poetry became her lost art, her talent hidden away in dusty notebooks, long forgotten and left to fade into silence.

For years, she played the game of life, moving up the ladder of success, tethered to a false dream spun from the web of societal lies. But the illusion shattered when her beloved nana and her mother died within years of each other, shaking Shayna's world to the core. Grief plunged her into the depths of despair, and darkness took hold of her. As she cried out toward death, antagonizing it even, something miraculous happened. She found herself in the darkness—the self she had abandoned, the voice that had been waiting in those forgotten notebooks.

A bit bewildered and intrigued, Shayna followed her heart, and the words began to flow once more. Pieces of her had been lost, but through her writing, so much more was found. With *The Flowers of Eden*, the first of five anticipated volumes in *The Awakening Rose Collection*, Shayna shares her journey to guide others on their own paths of healing and rediscovery.

The Flowers of Eden marks the beginning of an extraordinary journey, both for Shayna and her readers. As the first of five volumes, this book sets the stage for a deeper exploration of healing, resilience, and transformation. With each installment, Shayna is committed to guiding others through their own paths of self-discovery, offering words of comfort, hope, and empowerment along the way.

This collection is more than poetry—it's an invitation to reclaim the parts of ourselves we've forgotten, to embrace both our light and shadow, and to bloom into the fullness of who we are meant to be. The journey continues, and Shayna is honored to walk it with you.

www.ingramcontent.com/pod-product-compliance
Ingram Content Group UK Ltd.
Pitfield, Milton Keynes, MK11 3LW, UK
UKHW020047220125
453903UK00004B/24